D0904897

Brain Games
PICTURE PUZZLES

Edward Godwin

WINDMILL
BOOKS ™
NEW YORK

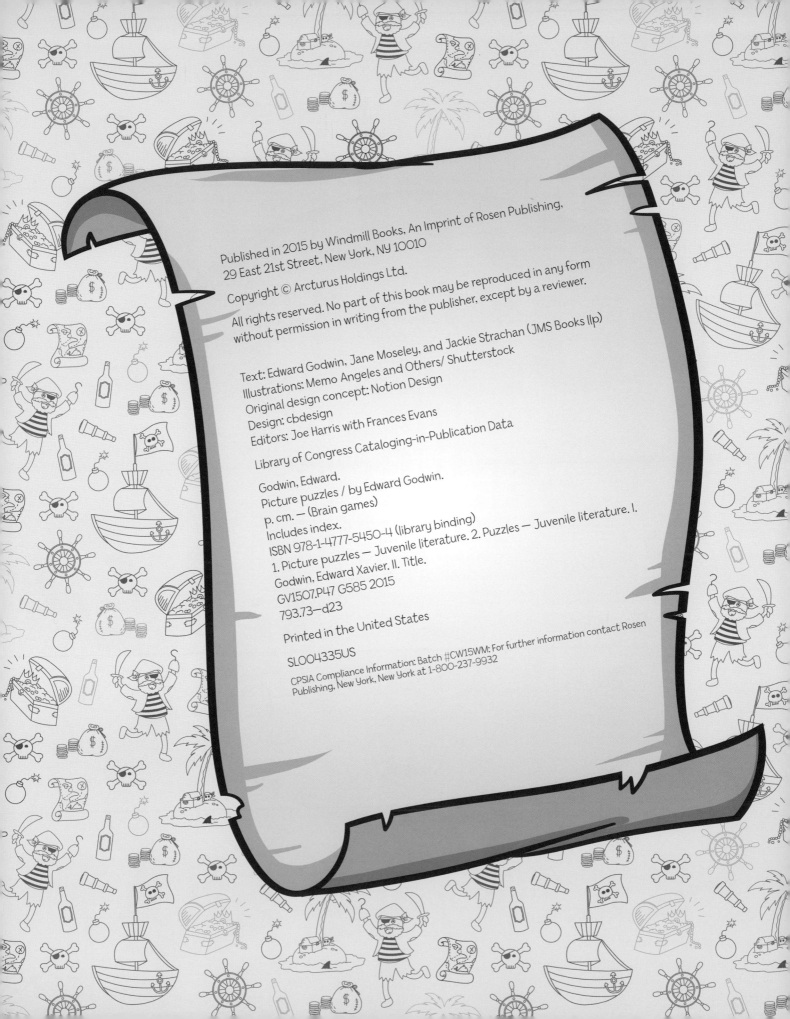

Published in 2015 by Windmill Books, An Imprint of Rosen Publishing,
29 East 21st Street, New York, NY 10010

Copyright © Arcturus Holdings Ltd.

Text: Edward Godwin, Jane Moseley, and Jackie Strachan (JMS Books llp)
Illustrations: Memo Angeles and Others/ Shutterstock
Original design concept: Notion Design
Design: cbdesign
Editors: Joe Harris with Frances Evans

Library of Congress Cataloging-in-Publication Data

Godwin, Edward.
Picture puzzles / by Edward Godwin.
p. cm. — (Brain games)
Includes index.
ISBN 978-1-4777-5450-4 (library binding)
1. Picture puzzles — Juvenile literature. 2. Puzzles — Juvenile literature. I. Godwin, Edward Xavier. II. Title.
GV1507.P47 G585 2015
793.73—d23

Printed in the United States

SL004335US

CPSIA Compliance Information: Batch #CW15WM: For further information contact Rosen Publishing, New York, New York at 1-800-237-9932

CONTENTS

PIRATE PUZZLER

Can you arrange these four coins so that each one is touching every other coin? Remember to check your answers in the back! (Tip: use some real coins to help find the answer!)

SHADOW MONSTER

Which shadow matches the monster exactly?

A

B

C

D

BIG BAD WOLF...

LOOKS LIKE RAIN

Can you spot which boot does not have a matching pair?

PAPYRUS POSER

Work out which number is represented by each symbol to make the sums add up in each row and column.

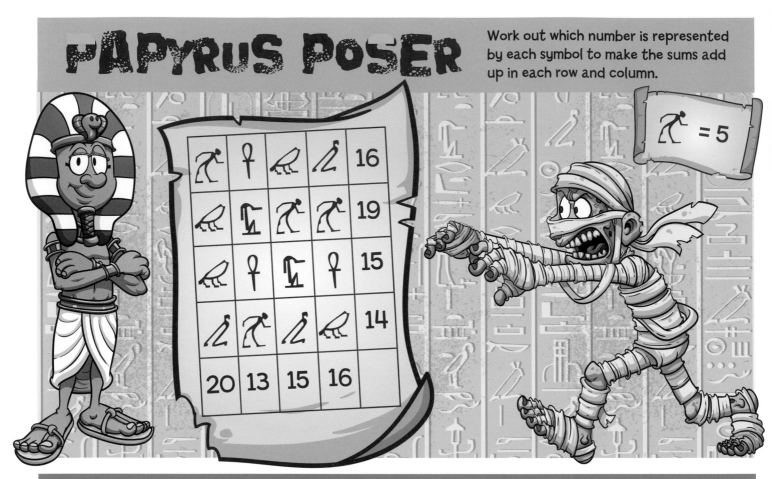

= 5

KING OF THE CASTLE!

Can you spot the rogue number in the windows?

CUPCAKE CONUNDRUM

Which cupcake belongs to Cindy? Use the clues to help you work it out.

1. It has a cherry on top.

2. It has chocolate icing.

3. It doesn't have sprinkles.

4. It doesn't have a red paper case.

GOING DOTTY

Five standard dice are shown in the pile on the right. What is the total number of dots on the sides you cannot see? (Clue: work out the sum of all the dots on the five dice first.)

Tip: the numbers on the cards represent their values, and ace = 1, jack = 11, queen = 12, and king = 13.

CARD SHARK

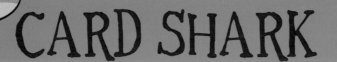

What playing card should complete the sequence?

PARROTS ON PATROL

Only two of these pirate parrots are exactly the same. Can you spot which two?

OVER THE RAINBOW

Turn this diamond shape into a triangle by moving just two coins.

Tip: use some real coins to help find the answer.

DIAMOND DIGGERS

Which group of gems is different to the rest?

THIS LITTLE PIGGY WENT TO MARKET...

Place the coins in the piggy banks to give the totals shown on their sides. Each coin can be used only once.

INTO THE DEEP

In each group of bubbles we have added a rogue number. Can you work out which one it is?

7 12 9 8 20 14 8 35 30 18 3 18 32 21 12 12 24 6 28 24

A   B   C   D

DRAGON'S HOARD

How many different sums of money can you make, each made up of two different coins?

1   5   10   20   25   50

PENCIL POWER

Move two pencils to make two squares. (Tip: use some real pencils to help find the answer!)

KEY QUESTION

Look at the shape of each key. Which one matches the treasure chest lock on the left?

Tip: the numbers on the cards represent their values, and ace = 1, jack = 11, queen = 12, and king = 13.

IT'S ON THE CARDS!

What playing card should take the place of the question mark in the sequence above?

11

BEWILDERING BOXES

When the figure below is folded to form a cube, just one of the four boxes on the left can be produced. Which one?

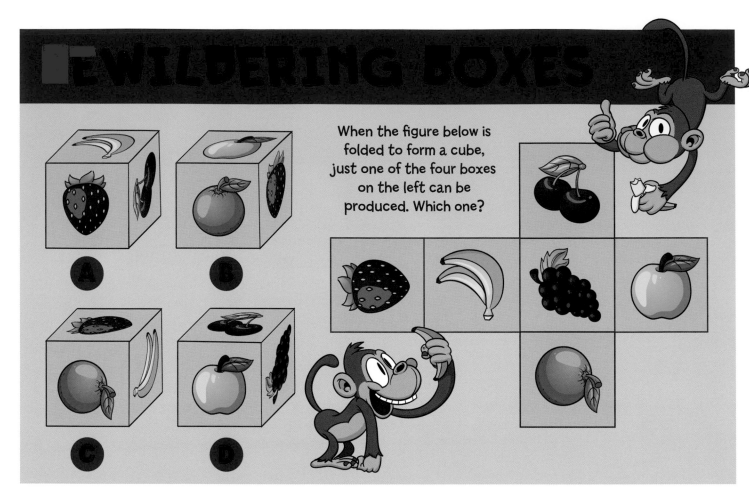

A

B

C

D

POSY POSER

Can you work out which two sets of flowers are identical?

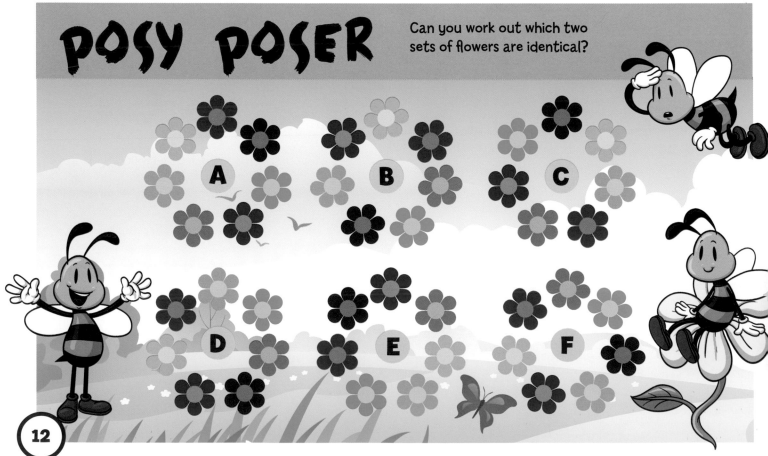

A

B

C

D

E

F

WINTER WONDERLAND

Can you find the matching pair of snowflakes hidden in this snow storm?

IT'S IN THE STARS

Using the first two stars as examples, work out which number is missing. Check your answers when you're done.

13

WHICH WITCH?

Which shadow matches the witch exactly?

A B C D E

TEACHER'S PET

Using the clues given, can you work out which pupil has just been named top of the class?

1. The student has red hair.

2. The student doesn't have black shoes.

3. The student doesn't have a blue shirt.

4. The student's name begins with "K."

Kitty   Amanda   Billy   Katie   Kevin   Kim

SILLY SAFARI

Which of these creatures is the odd one out and why? Clue: it's not the bat!

JUST SOCK IT TO ME

Can you spot which sock does not have a matching pair?

1   2   3   4   5   6   7   8   9   10   11   12   13   14   15

ROCK 'N' ROLL

From the muddled up letters, can you work out what creature is chasing the caveman?

EASTER BUNNY

Each easter egg has a matching pair except one. Can you spot it?

Which of the four alternatives below finishes the sequence? (Clue: start by looking at the yellow and blue keys ...)

PENCIL POWER

Move three pencils to make five triangles.
(Tip: use some real pencils to help find the answer!)

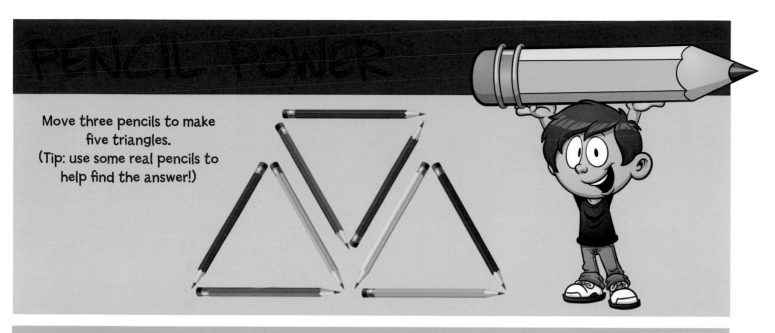

ANIMAL ANTICS

Can you work out which of these animals is the odd one out and why?

PLAY THE GAME

Find four games by rearranging the letters in each circle.

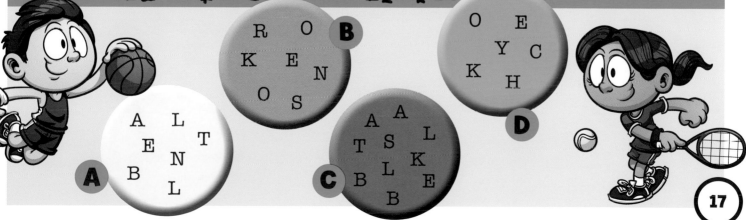

B — R O K E N O S

D — O E Y C K H

A — A L T E N L B

C — A A T S L K B B E

KOOKY COOKIES

Using the clues given, can you help Emma choose a cookie?

A **B** **C**

D **E** **F**

1. She doesn't want a plain one.

2. She's not in the mood for stripes.

3. She doesn't want choc chips.

4. She wants one with icing on it.

ART ATTACK!

Which of these colors is the odd one out and why?

Move four coins to make this downward-pointing arrow into an upward-pointing arrow.

Tip: use some real coins to help find the answer.

PENNY PINCHER

FRACTION FUN

Which sports shirt should each player wear?

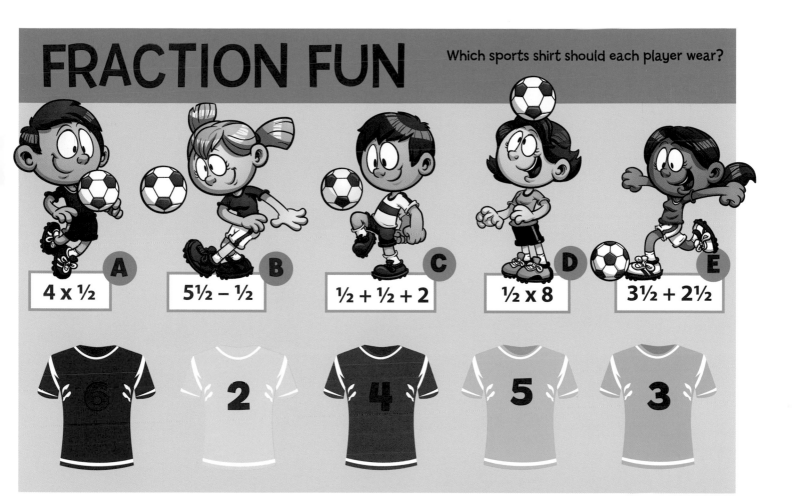

A $4 \times \frac{1}{2}$

B $5\frac{1}{2} - \frac{1}{2}$

C $\frac{1}{2} + \frac{1}{2} + 2$

D $\frac{1}{2} \times 8$

E $3\frac{1}{2} + 2\frac{1}{2}$

6 2 4 5 3

DINO DISCOVERY

The names of these dinosaurs have been muddled up. Can you work out what they are?

A T N U R S A E Y R U R O S X A N

B P L O C E Y R D T T A

C A T S S S G R E U U O

EURO ZONE

Can you rearrange the letters to spell out the four European countries that the children come from?

ON THE BALL

The names of four sports are muddled up on these balls. Can you work out which ones they are?

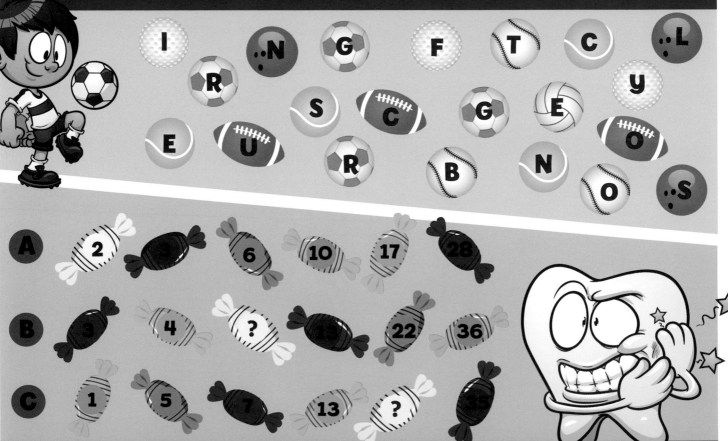

A 2 3 6 10 17 28

B 3 4 ? 13 22 36

C 1 5 7 13 ? 35

SWEET TOOTH!

Put on your thinking caps and work out which number is missing from each row of candy. Use the first line as an example.

APPLE TEASER

Can you work out which number completes this sequence of apples? (Clue: a times table might be useful here.)

1 3 7 13 21 31 43

THIS LITTLE PIGGY STAYED AT HOME...

Place the coins in the piggy banks to give the totals shown on their sides. Each coin can be used only once.

A — 0.98
B — 1.43
C — 0.86

WILD WEST HERO

Using the top two stars as an example, find the missing number.

PUZZLING PIGGIES

Only two of these pigs are exactly the same. Can you spot which two?

PLAY YOUR CARDS RIGHT...

Leaving 12 of the 16 cards exactly where they are, change the positions (but not the values) of four cards so that the values in each row, column, and the two long diagonal lines total exactly 41. Any value card can appear more than once in the same row, column, or line.

The numbers on the cards represent their values, and ace = 1, jack = 11, queen = 12, and king = 13.

(Tip: the cards in the diagonal lines already add up to 41.)

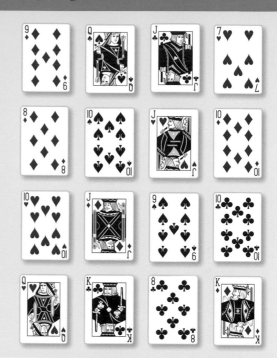

FAMILY PORTRAIT

Can you work out which member of the family is the odd one out and why?

ME AND MY SHADOW

Which shadow matches the wizard exactly?

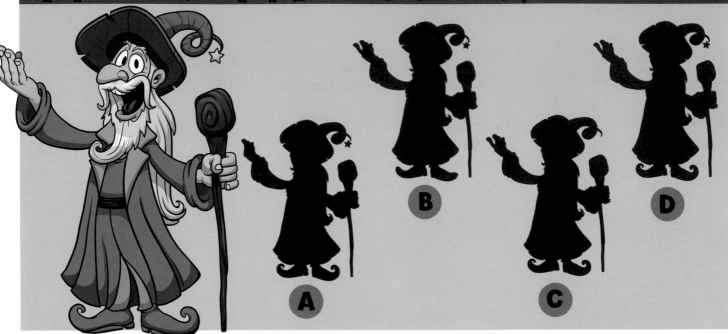

BURIED TREASURE

Follow the directions to work out where the treasure is hidden.

1 Starting in square B5, walk north for 4 squares.
2 Move 2 squares to the east.
3 Head south for 3 squares.
4 Walk west for 3 squares.
5 Step 1 square to the north.
6 Travel east for 2 squares.

ON VACATION

Using the labels on the cases as clues, can you work out the cities and the countries our traveller has visited?

"SPOT" THE DIFFERENCE

Only two of these clowns are exactly the same. Can you spot which ones?

THIS LITTLE PIGGY CRIED ALL THE WAY HOME!

Place the coins in the piggy banks to give the totals shown on their sides. Each coin can be used only once.

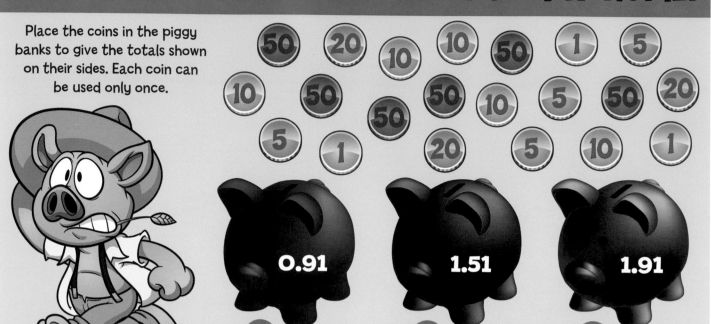

0.91

A

1.51

B

1.91

C

HEAVENS ABOVE

Can you unscramble the letters to find the name of each planet? Remember to check your answers!

A — UTRJIPE

B — SNUVEE

C — URANSTN

D — CRYEUMR

E — ETENPENU

F — SNRUUA

G — ASRM

26

FARMYARD FUN

Which of these animals is the odd one out and why? (Tip: think about the kind of food they like!)

GIFT WRAPPED!

Can you find the missing number? (Tip: try looking at the boxes from all directions.)

CUCKOO IN THE NEST

Can you work out which number egg is the odd one out in each nest?

ANSWERS

page 4

PIRATE PUZZLER

SHADOW MONSTER
Answer = **C**
(A has no scales on his tail; B has a smaller tip to his tail; D has no ears.)

page 5

BIG BAD WOLF...
Answer = **47**
Double each number and add 1 to get the next.

LOOKS LIKE RAIN
Answer = **16**

page 6

PAPYRUS POSER

⚲ = **3**

🦜 = **7**

🦢 = **1**

🏑 = **2**

KING OF THE CASTLE!
Answer = **4**
All the other numbers are odd.

page 7

CUPCAKE CONUNDRUM
Answer = **F**

GOING DOTTY
Answer = **73**
The sum of all the dots on five dice is 105; you can see 32 dots, so the remaining number is 73.

CARD SHARK
Answer = **king of hearts**
The values rise by two each time and the suits repeat in the order clubs, diamonds, hearts, spades.

page 8

PARROTS ON PATROL
Answer = **A** and **E**
(B is missing his earring; C has a black belt buckle; D is missing the bones on his hat.)

OVER THE RAINBOW
The coins that have moved are shown as dotted outlines.

page 9

DIAMOND DIGGERS
Answer = **E**
In all of the others, the sequence red, orange, yellow, green, blue, indigo, and violet can be seen in a clockwise direction.

THIS LITTLE PIGGY WENT TO MARKET...

A = 50, 50, 50, 10, 5, 1, 1, 1

B = 50, 20, 20, 1, 1, 1

C = 50, 50, 50, 50, 20, 1

page 10

INTO THE DEEP

A = **7**
All the rest are multiples of 3

B = **8**
All the rest are multiples of 6

C = **32**
All the rest are multiples of 7

D = **18**
All the rest are multiples of 4

DRAGON'S HOARD

Answer = **15**
Here are the different combinations:

1 + 5 = 6	5 + 50 = 55
1 + 10 = 11	10 + 20 = 30
1 + 20 = 21	10 + 25 = 35
1 + 25 = 26	10 + 50 = 60
1 + 50 = 51	20 + 25 = 45
5 + 10 = 15	20 + 50 = 70
5 + 20 = 25	25 + 50 = 75
5 + 25 = 30	

page 11

PENCIL POWER

The pencils that have been moved are shown as dotted lines.

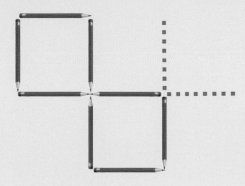

KEY QUESTION

Answer = **D**

IT'S ON THE CARDS!

Answer = **nine of diamonds**
The values change by minus 3, plus 2, minus 4, plus 3, minus 5, plus 4, and the suits repeat in the order hearts, clubs, diamonds, spades.

page 12

BEWILDERING BOXES

Answer = **B**
Look carefully at the position of the fruit!

POSY POSER

Answer = **B** and **F**

page 13

WINTER WONDERLAND

Answer = **6** and **15**

IT'S IN THE STARS

Answer = **15**
Add up the outer numbers and divide by 2 to get the middle numbers.

page 14

WHICH WITCH?

Answer = **D**
(In A the end of the witch's hat is pointing upward; in B her feet are not pointing down; in C the front end of the broom is shortened; in E the cat has no tail.)

TEACHER'S PET

Answer = **Katie**

page 15

SILLY SAFARI

Answer = **chameleon** (a reptile)
All the other animals are mammals.

JUST SOCK IT TO ME

Answer = **13**

ROCK 'N' ROLL

Answer = **Saber Tooth Tiger**

page 16

EASTER BUNNY
Answer = **12**

KEY TO SUCCESS
Answer = **D**
The outer keys move one place counterclockwise each time, and the inner key rotates by 180 degrees, as do the blue, gray, and red keys.

page 17

PENCIL POWER
The pencils that have been moved are shown as dotted lines. They make one big triangle and four smaller triangles.

ANIMAL ANTICS
Answer = **parrot**
It is the only animal that can fly.

PLAY THE GAME
A = **Netball**
B = **Snooker**
C = **Basketball**
D = **Hockey**

page 18

KOOKY COOKIES
Answer = **E**

ART ATTACK!
Answer = **Brown**
It is the only one of the colors that does not feature in the rainbow.

PENNY PINCHER
The coins that have moved are shown as dotted outlines.

page 19

FRACTION FUN
A = **2**
B = **5**
C = **3**
D = **4**
E = **6**

DINO DISCOVERY
A = **Tyrannosaurus Rex**
B = **Pterodactyl**
C = **Stegosaurus**

page 20

EURO ZONE
A = France
B = Denmark
C = Germany
D = Portugal

ON THE BALL
Golf, tennis, soccer, rugby.

SWEET TOOTH!
Row B = **8**
Row C = **21**
In each row, add the first two numbers together and add 1 to give the next number along.

page 21

APPLE TEASER
Answer = **57**
Moving from left to right, use your 2 times table at every step. Add 2, then 4, then 6, and so on.

THIS LITTLE PIGGY STAYED AT HOME...
A = 50, 20, 20, 5, 1, 1, 1
B = 50, 50, 20, 20, 1, 1, 1
C = 50, 10, 10, 5, 5, 5, 1

page 22

WILD WEST HERO
Answer = **9**
Add up the outer numbers and divide the result by 3 to get the middle numbers.

PUZZLING PIGGIES
Answer = **C** and **D**
(A is missing the pocket on his overalls; B has yellow spots on his bag; E has no tail; F has a yellow cap.)

page 23

PLAY YOUR CARDS RIGHT...
The cards that have moved are shown with dotted outlines.

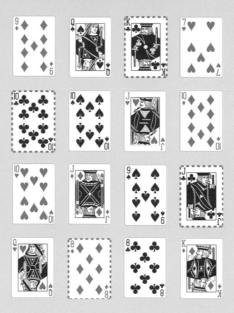

FAMILY PORTRAIT
Answer = **Father**
All the rest are female relatives.

page 24

ME AND MY SHADOW
Answer = **D**
(A's finger is missing; the ends of B's slippers are not curly; C's hat does not have a star.)

BURIED TREASURE
Answer = **C3**

page 25

ON VACATION
A = **Athens, Greece**
B = **Rome, Italy**
C = **Paris, France**
D = **New York, USA**

"SPOT" THE DIFFERENCE
Answer = **B** and **E**

page 26

THIS LITTLE PIGGY CRIED ALL THE WAY HOME!
A = **50, 20, 10, 5, 5, 1**
B = **50, 50, 20, 10, 10, 10, 1**
C = **50, 50, 50, 20, 10, 5, 5, 1**

HEAVENS ABOVE
A = **Jupiter**
B = **Venus**
C = **Saturn**
D = **Mercury**
E = **Neptune**
F = **Uranus**
G = **Mars**

page 27

FARMYARD FUN
Answer = **Dog**
It is the only meat-eater.

GIFT WRAPPED!
Answer = **5**
The numbers create a magic square, in which the numbers along any vertical, horizontal, or diagonal line add up to 15.

CUCKOO IN THE NEST
Nest A = **8** All the other numbers are multiples of 3.
Nest B = **10** All the other numbers are multiples of 4.

GLOSSARY

bewildering (bih-WILL-duhr-ing) Very confusing and difficult to work out.

card shark (KAHRD-shahrk) A card player who makes a living by cheating at card games.

conundrum (cun-UM-drum) A riddle or puzzle.

cuckoo (KOO-koo) A bird that lays its eggs in the nests of other birds.

hoard (HOHRD) A hidden supply or store.

identical (y-DENT-ik-ul) Exactly alike or equal.

papyrus (puh-PY-rus) A document written on paper made from the papyrus plant, used by ancient Egyptians.

rogue (ROHG) Behaving in a way that is not expected.

safari (su-FAH-ree) A journey into the wild to see animals, especially in eastern Africa.

sequence (SEE-kwens) An arrangement of things in a particular order.

wonderland (WUN-duhr-land) An imaginary place full of beauty and charm.

FURTHER READING

Harbin-Miles, Ruth, Don Balka, and Ted Hull. *Math Games.* Huntington Beach, CA. Shell Education, 2013.

Stickels, Terry. *Math Puzzles and Brainteasers, Grades 3—5.* San Francisco, CA. Jossey-Bass, 2009.

Tang, Greg. *Math-terpieces: The Art of Problem Solving.* New York, NY. Scholastic, 2013.

WEB SITES

For web resources related to the subject of this book, go to:

www. windmillbooks.com/weblinks and select this book's title.

INDEX